ANCIENT ISRAEL

CASPIAN
SEA

ASSYRIA

•Nineveh

RAM

Euphrates River

Tigris River

BA   ONIA

Babylon•

AB

Ur

PERSIAN GULF

N

ARABIA

FOREWORD
Cal Jernigan, Senior Pastor

WHAT YOU HOLD IN YOUR HANDS is simply the greatest story ever told! It is a story that has been cherished all throughout time and to this very day people long to know and understand it. If you take the time to get to know what is written in these pages, your story will make more sense than you've ever imagined! Just as an actor needs to read the whole script before his character's role makes sense, so understanding it will answer a myriad of questions you've always wanted answered regarding your story.

I want to invite you to join us on an adventure – getting to know this incredible story! I believe doing so is the greatest investment of time one could ever make. You see, this is the story of a Creator God, the very people He created, and just how far this God will go to bless His creation. You'll come to understand that your journey in this life is very much a part of His Story!

So, what's the best way to discover all this?

- First, make a commitment to **READ** one chapter every week.

- Second, from now until we complete this book, decide to attend church every weekend! When you do, you will **HEAR** a message that is directly related to the chapter you have just read. You will understand what you are hearing like never before.

- And third, commit to **DISCUSS** what you have read and heard with others who are also making the same discoveries you are making. At Central we have an extensive network of Life Groups that gather every week for this very purpose. Not only will you learn a great deal by doing this, you will probably make some of the best friends you have ever had.

I am absolutely confident that God will bless all who make knowing this story a priority. It's an adventure waiting to happen. It's an adventure designed for you!

I am looking forward to making incredible memories together as we discover what makes this the greatest story ever!

Cal Jernigan

FIND
YOUR
COMMUNITY

WELCOME to
CENTRAL CHRISTIAN CHURCH

(Me) **MESA CAMPUS**—Lindsay Rd. & Brown Rd.

(Gi) **GILBERT CAMPUS**—Lindsay Rd. & Germann Rd.

(Qc) **QUEEN CREEK CAMPUS**—Ocotillo Rd. & Rittenhouse Rd.

(Gl) **GLENDALE CAMPUS**—Glendale Ave. & 83rd Ave.

(Ah) **AHWATUKEE CAMPUS**—48th St. & Chandler Blvd.

(♀) **NORTH AFRICA**—Globally we are focused on one of the largest segments of people who are still unreached with the gospel. **CentralAZ.com/GO**

CONTINUE THE DISCUSSION
Continue the discussion online at **CentralAZ.com/Blog**

CONNECTION CARD
Use this card to stay connected with Central. First-time or recent guest, bring this card to Starting Point in the lobby for a gift.

SERMON COMPANION
Dive deeper into this week's message with the sermon companion. Visit **CentralAZ.com/SermonCompanion** to download.

MISS A WEEK?
Watch messages online at **CentralAZ.com/Messages**

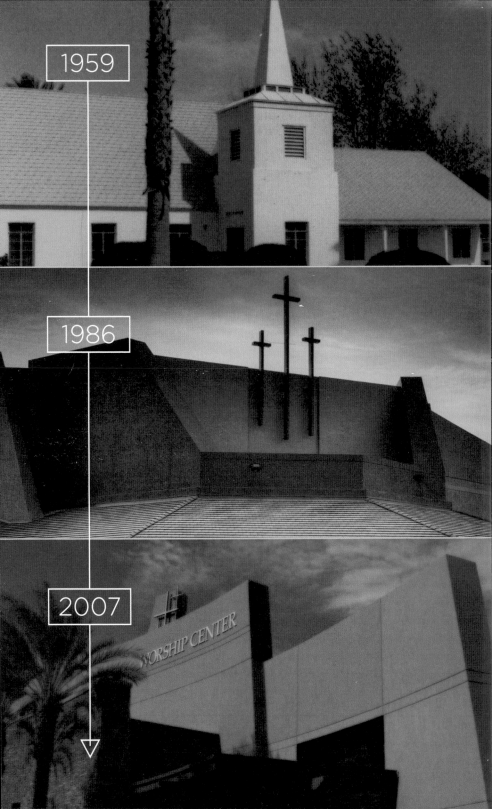

1959

1986

2007

WORSHIP CENTER

CENTRAL
HISTORY

Some of the most well-known organizations today came from small and humble beginnings, and Central Christian Church is no exception.

In spring of 1959, a father and son were returning from a fishing trip when they noticed a "For Sale" sign on the Church of the Nazarene in Mesa. "Wouldn't that be a good place to start a Christian Church?" the son remarked to his dad. "Yes," he replied, "somebody ought to do something about it."

Just three short months later the son, Joe Carson Smith, answered the call to "do something about it" and became the first pastor of Central Christian Church. Opening its doors in July of 1959, Central hosted 37 people on average, largely due to Joe's door-to-door invites.

As the attendance grew, however, Central outgrew its single acre and moved onto a 6 ½ acre property, seeing the retirement of Pastor Smith and greeting Charles Cook, a pastor known for his experience growing churches. In his ten years at Central the attendance more than doubled growing to a size of 400 people worshipping together each Sunday.

In April of 1979, Central greeted Dr. LeRoy Lawson as the new senior pastor. In 1982, under Roy's leadership, Central purchased 33 acres on Lindsay and Brown. Back then, nobody had ever heard of a mega church, and purchasing so much land confused the public. But Central had a good reason—with 33 acres, we would never have to buy land again! God continued to grow his church and by the time Roy wrapped up his ministry in 1999, the church had grown to 4000 people.

Because of this, Central's 33 acres quickly became too small. Under the new senior pastor, Cal Jernigan, Central started to look for a new location where even more people could worship together. In 2001, Central closed escrow on a 160 acre plot of land in Gilbert. Through a series of events that were nothing short of miraculous, the Gilbert campus opened in 2007. Now Central became a church that met on multiple sites and was significantly impacting more than just one city.

Well, this pattern has continued and now, in addition to Mesa and Gilbert, there are Central campuses in Queen Creek, Glendale, and Ahwatukee. These days, each and every weekend, 10,000 people gather together to experience the worship and teaching ministry of Central.

It has been 55 years since Central Christian Church started, but we are confident our story is only just beginning! In the past, God blessed the faith of so many people to build this church into what it is today. Yet we believe this is just the foundation upon which God will build his church for the future. The coolest part of all is that we believe you were meant to be a part of this story! The future begins now!

OUR

CORE
VALUES

PRAYER

As a community of believers, we seek God's guidance and direction through prayer in all that we do as a church and in all aspects of our daily lives.

ALL PEOPLE

We primarily exist for the sake of those who are not yet part of the Body of Christ, intending to mature all believers into fully transformed, committed, and reproducing followers of Christ.

THE BIBLE

We acknowledge the Bible as the revealed truth of God, providing direction for our lives. We desire to communicate its truth in a manner that relates to our culture.

AUTHENTICITY

This is a place of grace and forgiveness where everyone is allowed, encouraged, and expectd to be authentic; but this is also a place where complacency is challenged. Come as you are and grow in your faith.

INVOLVEMENT

Every believer within this community is responsible to use his or her spiritual gifts, time, energy, and finances for honoring God through ministry.

FUTURE GENERATIONS

We are a community where children and youth are highly valued; we sacrificially share the responsiblity of raising godly children and youth.

THERE
IS
MORE
TO
LIFE
THAN
ME

LUKE 9:23

WWW.CENTRALAZ.COM

f 🐦 v /CENTRALAZ

CENTRALAZ.COM/BLOG

Join the conversation:
#TheStorySeries